ON EA(

by Ha

GW00832240

On Eagles' Wings

A CHRISTIAN PERSPECTIVE

ON M.E.

by

HAZEL STAPLETON

2002

Quinta Press

Weston Rhyn

Quinta Press

Meadow View, Quinta Crescent, Weston Rhyn, Oswestry, Shropshire, England, SY10 7RN

Visit our web-site:
http://www.quintapress.com

ISBN 1 89785613 X

Printed by Quinta Business Services

'... but those who hope in
the Lord will renew their strength.
They will soar on wings like eagles...'

ISAIAH 40:31 (N.I.V.)

CONTENTS

Page

Leave all your troubles in the hands
Of God Who guides us all,
And never doubt He understands
Your worries, large and small.
And as He leads you day by day
Remaining always near,
May you be blessed in many ways
And daily given cheer.
(Ahlene Fitch)

WHAT IS M.E.?

So you have got M.E.. Or you know someone who has it. You are not alone—even though you may feel it! M.E. now affects at least 170,000 people in this country, probably many more, and cases of M.E. now well out-number those of M.S. (multiple sclerosis).

M.E. stands for Myalgic Encephalomyelitis. It is basically a multi-system failure, and is often classed as a neurological illness. It brings with it muscle fatigue, flu-like symptoms, digestive problems, exhaustion which is not alleviated by rest, as well as many other problems which can vary from person to person. It affects the central nervous system, muscles, immune and digestive systems, and is listed by the World Health Organization as a neurological condition.

M.E. is also known as PVFS (Post-Viral Fatigue Syndrome), is a type of C.F.S. (Chronic Fatigue Syndrome), and in America it is known as C.F.I.D.S.—Chronic Fatigue and Immune Dysfunction Syndrome. Many people now actually refer to the illness as C.F.S.—but this is unfortunate, as firstly, C.F.S. is really an 'umbrella' term covering a number of fatigue syndromes. Secondly, the term C.F.S. does tend to trivialize the illness by giving the impression that fatigue is the only problem faced by those who have it, which is certainly not the case!

It is important to realize that M.E. should not be confused with a post-viral debility, which normally lasts for just a few weeks after a virus, but can leave a person feeling low for 2 or 3 months.

When I first became ill in February 1991, M.E. was something I'd only vaguely heard of— I knew that it was an illness, but my knowledge of it consisted of thinking that it was 'something to do with a virus'! Due to the increase in awareness of the illness over the past few years, most people now at least recognize that M.E. is a serious illness, even if they know very little about it.

The cause of M.E. is largely unknown, although there are various theories. It does seem that there are some people who are more likely to develop the illness than others—particularly those aged 20–40 years old working in occupations where they are regularly exposed to a variety of viral infections *e.g.* health workers and teachers.

More often than not the illness follows a virus, but the actual trigger of M.E. is also unknown, although it does appear that stress could be a factor—not just mental stress, but physical stresses such as infections, injuries, over-use of broad spectrum antibiotics, a bad diet, environmental pollution, vaccinations, pesticides, etc. Lessening exposure to these stresses could lessen the chances of a person developing M.E.—although unfortunately there are always exceptions to the rule!

Once a person has M.E. it is possible that there are certain factors which could hinder recovery and help prolong the condition *e.g.* persistent infections, immune system disturbance, candida overgrowth, vitamin and mineral deficiencies, allergies and intolerances (the most common food intolerances being to dairy and gluten containing products), and depression (as a result of M.E., not as its cause). Dealing with these factors could well help with recovery from M.E.

Research has shown that in people with M.E. there is:

- damage to muscle tissue. Biopsies show clear evidence of structural damage to the mitochondria, indicating the possibility of biochemical problems in the muscle cells.

- lesions in the brain, probably caused by inflammation. S.P.E.C.T. scans (Single Photon Emission Computed Tomography—radionuclide scanning) show that there is reduced blood flow to some parts of the brain as well as evidence of central nervous system dysfunction. These findings differ from those in people with depressive illnesses—which is a problem for those who believe that M.E. is a form of depression!

- evidence of an overactive immune system—consistent with a persistent infection.

- a number of disturbances in the hypothalamus.

- neuropsychological abnormalities consistent with an organic brain disorder, similar to the problems found in M.S. patients.

- M.E. is more common in women than in men, but the reason for this is unknown.

A diagnosis of M.E. is not normally considered unless activity levels are reduced by at least 50%. As there is not yet a test for M.E., it is usually made on the presence of certain symptoms, along with tests to exclude other possibilities, many of which have similar symptoms to M.E. (*e.g.* glandular fever, M.S., some cancers, hypo-thyroid problems, other neurological conditions).

Many doctors will not diagnose M.E. until a person has been unwell for 6 months (in order to rule out other conditions and prove the chronic nature of the problem), although some will do so after 3 months.

M.E. affects mainly the muscles, the brain and the nerves, as is shown in its name— myalgic (muscles); encephalo (brain); myelitis (nerves). The term 'Myalgic Encephalomyelitis' may not be technically 100% correct, in that there is little evidence of brain and spinal cord inflammation present, but many of the symptoms are what would be expected if there was inflammation present. The name also helps to convey the seriousness of the condition, and is preferable to C.F.S.!

The main diagnostic symptoms of M.E. are as follows:

1 *Fatigue*—Fatigue is the principal symptom of the illness, is experienced by all sufferers, and must not have previously been a problem. It is caused by trivially small exertion—physical or mental—compared to before the onset of the illness. Activity can put someone in bed for days or, if overdone, can cause a major relapse. The reaction to activity can be immediate or be delayed by as much as 72 hours, which can make planning anything very difficult.

The exhaustion in M.E. is severe, disabling, and totally unlike that experienced by healthy people—some have described it as being totally drained of energy and 'having their plug pulled out'. Unlike normal tiredness it is not helped by exercise and would be made worse by it.

2 *Cognitive Problems and Psychoneurological Disturbances*—such as impairment of concentration and short-term memory;

mixing-up of words; disturbed, unrefreshing sleep, with a lack of normal 'restorative' sleep; balance problems; emotional lability.

3 *Unpredictable Fluctuation of Symptoms*—from day to day, or within a day. This can mean not feeling tired all the time, but it is common to feel ill all the time! Symptoms can be exacerbated by doing too much and not managing the condition properly.

Other symptoms can often include: muscle pain (which can be severe) and muscle weakness; multi-joint pain, normally without swelling; clinical/laboratory evidence of viral infection, with sore throats and painful lymph nodes; poor temperature control *i.e.* sweating or shivering; altered sleep patterns; chest pain (which should be investigated if frequent and/or severe); abnormalities to the heart rate and rhythm, including palpitations; anxiety and/or panic attacks; visual disturbances; problems with digestion similar to Irritable Bowel Syndrome; mood swings, which can make the person quite unpredictable; severe migraine-type headaches; and generally feeling unwell.

Depression is fairly common, but is an effect and *not* a cause of M.E. The percentage of those with M.E. who are diagnosed with clinical depression (as opposed to just feeling 'fed-up') is no different than what would be expected in any chronic illness, *e.g.* as in M.S.

These symptoms could, of course, be caused by a number of illnesses, and therefore only help to confirm the diagnosis when the three 'diagnostic symptoms' have all been present for a minimum of three months. However, most people with M.E. don't have all the symptoms (well, not all at one time anyway!), and the symptoms themselves can vary from day to day.

M.E. usually has a sudden onset following an infectious illness (*e.g.* flu, gastroenteritis), but some sufferers find that it has a slow onset with no particular starting point. It can also follow the use of pesticides/organo-phosphates or a vaccination—as in my case, where my illness was started by a Hepatitis B vaccine which I was required to have as a student nurse. Needless to say, the onset of M.E. brought my brief nursing career to an abrupt end!

At best people with M.E. manage to work, even if they have to spend every evening and weekend resting. Some, however, are confined to the house, or even to bed; while others are somewhere in the middle—not housebound, yet unable to work. M.E. often lasts for years, and as yet there is no known cure.

It is thought that about 80% of people with M.E. recover to some degree in time. Approximately 20% make a full recovery with no after-effects and are able to lead normal lives. 60% recover up to a certain point, but never regain full health and have to live within certain limits—such as sticking to particular diets, working on a part-time basis and carefully pacing themselves. Unfortunately the other 20% may become permanently disabled by their condition and find themselves very dependent on others in order to manage from day to day. At its very worst M.E. can be fatal—but this is rare, and usually due to complications such as an additional infection which weakens the heart.

Those who make the best progress tend to be those who get an early diagnosis and so learn to manage the illness properly, with the help and support of their G.P., family and friends. Children, especially, do tend to make good recoveries, even if severely affected for a number of years.

Hopefully as awareness and understanding

of M.E. increases the percentage of those making a full recovery will also increase. Unfortunately for some it can take months or even years to obtain a firm diagnosis. During the intervening time they push themselves too hard—possibly resulting in long-term damage which could have been avoided with early diagnosis and management advice.

The length of illness varies considerably. For some it is relatively short (*i.e.* less than two years), whilst for others it is a lot longer. However if you have M.E. it is not a good idea to compare yourself too much with other sufferers, as once you have M.E. it is a very individual illness, with different people experiencing different problems. Just because some people have M.E. for four or five years doesn't mean that you will—there are things that you can do which will help you to manage your condition properly and improve your chances of recovery. Remember, even if you have been ill for years, don't give up! It is never too late to start learning how to manage the illness, and it is possible to make good progress even after many years.

Most people with M.E. find that there are certain things that cause their symptoms to worsen, resulting in a relapse in their condition *e.g.* stress, exercise, further infections, anaesthetics, antibiotics, vaccinations, pesticides, and alcohol.

One of the characteristics of M.E. is its fluctuating nature, with patterns of good and bad stages. Those with M.E. often find that they are turned from active, independent people into those who are dependent on others, unable to live their lives as they did before the onset of their illness. This on its own can cause a loss of self-confidence—and friends and relatives of those with M.E. should, where possible, give help and encouragement to boost the confidence of the sufferer. However, compared with those who suffer from depressive illness, people with M.E. tend to retain good motivation and appreciation of life.

A word of caution: M.E. is normally an 'unseen' illness, and in my experience this means that it is virtually impossible for people in general to understand and appreciate the impact and seriousness of the condition—unless they have either had it themselves or have a very close friend/relative with it. Trying to explain the crippling fatigue and severe pain is extremely difficult—in fact, most people seem surprised to know that pain is involved at all, as M.E. is thought by many to consist purely of fatigue!

As a result, I don't think that it is worth spending a great deal of time and energy trying to get people to understand the illness—as on the whole, they won't! By all means encourage the people you know to read up on M.E.—but don't expect too much! I am always happy to give information about the illness to anyone who is interested enough to ask for it, but other than that I feel that it is best to accept that it is a condition which is difficult enough to understand by those of us with it, and therefore almost impossible for those with no personal experience of it.

However, whilst from a human point of view it can be very difficult to find anyone who understands the problems of M.E., as a Christian I know that I have a Father in Heaven Who understands completely—God knows exactly what we are going through! He is sovereign, and it is a great source of joy and comfort to know that my life is in His hands— and of course, this is true for all who are Christians, who know Jesus Christ as their Saviour and Lord.

Also, we know from the Bible that during His time on earth the Lord Jesus knew what it was like to feel pain, to feel weak and tired. We are told in Hebrews 4:15 that 'we do not have a High Priest Who cannot sympathize with our weaknesses, but was in all points tempted as we are, yet without sin.' Surely this is another source of immense comfort to us, and means that we can 'come boldly to the throne of grace, that we may obtain mercy and find grace to help in time of need' (Hebrews 4:16)— whatever our circumstances may be! What a privilege! 'The Lord is my portion, says my soul, Therefore I hope in Him!' (Lamentations 3:24).

WHAT CAN I DO ABOUT M.E.?

Early diagnosis and management of M.E. are probably the two most important things for anyone with the condition, so therefore if you have (or if you think you have) got M.E., then the first thing to do is to get an early diagnosis. Sadly, this is often easier said than done! You will need to find a G.P. who is sympathetic, not one who tells you that 'it is all in the mind and you should pull yourself together'.

If your G.P. does not want to help, then it would be worth changing to one who does. Some parts of the country are better than others when it comes to finding doctors/practitioners who understand M.E.

You will be able to find out about sympathetic G.P.s in your area from other M.E. sufferers, and the charity Action for M.E., which has a list of consultants and G.P.s that have been recommended by others with the illness. If your G.P. is not helpful, or not very knowledgeable about M.E., you could try giving him some information about the condition. Both the M.E. Association and Action for M.E. have produced literature especially for doctors.

Although your G.P. probably won't know a lot about M.E., he can refer you to a specialist who will be able to confirm your diagnosis and give you further advice. Fortunately it does seem that the medical profession as a whole is becoming more aware of M.E. and is at last starting to take it seriously—although there is still a long way to go, and some doctors still do not recognise the condition.

The reason why an early diagnosis of M.E. is necessary is so that you can learn as much as possible about the illness and how to manage it—in order to increase your likelihood of recovery. It may be necessary to try certain drugs to relieve specific symptoms, and to consider changes to your diet and lifestyle.

Joining a local self-help group may also be useful.

Without an early diagnosis you will probably be advised to undergo various treatments/therapies that could well make your condition worse *e.g.* exercise programmes to 'help build up the muscles'—this would, more than likely, cause your condition to worsen. Some people are advised to try 'Cognitive Behaviour Therapy'—but this has only been found to be of any use in patients suffering from true depression as well as M.E.

The best person who can help you is yourself! It is a good idea to find out everything you can about M.E.—read books, magazines, leaflets. Although there is no cure for M.E. there are things that you can do that will help. You should also encourage family and friends to read up on M.E. as well, so that they can appreciate your problems more fully.

1. *Rest*—there are many so-called 'treatments' for M.E., some of which can be helpful, but the only one agreed on by everybody is rest. Rest, especially in the early stages of the illness or during a relapse, increases the chances of recovery as well as the recovery rate. Rest should be seen as a positive

treatment for M.E., not as just 'giving up'. As soon as you start to feel tired—mentally or physically—you should stop what you are doing. Going on to the point of exhaustion could mean taking weeks or months getting over a relapse, rather than hours or days.

Some people (especially doctors) feel that too much rest can lead to muscle wasting. Whilst it is true that as a result of resting muscles can become weak, there is no evidence of actual wasting. Most people with M.E. are able to keep up at least some movement around the house, or even take short walks. However, if completely bed-bound, some gentle, passive physiotherapy may be helpful—as long as the physiotherapist (or whoever carries it out) is sympathetic to the situation and has some understanding of the illness.

Having M.E. may well mean reorganizing your lifestyle and putting certain things 'on hold' until your health improves. It is very hard for most people to let go of things that they have been doing for years *e.g.* careers, hobbies, church activities, etc—but sometimes it is the only way to manage the illness and increase the possibility of recovery. You have to learn to say 'No'!

It is a good idea to try and establish a daily routine—if you are at your best in the morning, then that is the time to carry out daily activities. If your best time is in the evening, then there is little point trying to work in the morning!

Many people with M.E. have found it helpful to plan a certain time each day when they can rest *e.g.* in the afternoons—and it's a good idea (and often essential!) to let friends know when you rest, so that they will not interrupt you. One thing that I have found invaluable over the past few years is having a phone next to my bed—so that if I am the only one in the house when it rings, I don't have to get up to answer it!

If you do have a busy day, try and keep the next day or two free to 'catch up' on resting. Learn how to relax—quiet music is often helpful. Some people find themselves permanently exhausted—and this is normally due to trying to do too much. Whilst it is tempting to try and keep working, even on a part-time basis, for many this is just not possible, and will only result in worsening and/or prolonging the illness. For those who keep pushing themselves to work it often comes as a relief when they cut down/stop, begin to allow themselves to rest, and start to make some progress.

Obviously the best form of rest is sleep! Some sufferers say that they sleep too much—this is wrong, as it is probably the best thing that you can do, particularly in the early stages of the illness or during a relapse. Unfortunately, it is often the case that although feeling totally exhausted it is difficult to sleep at all—due to aches and pains, muscles twitching, panic attacks, breathing difficulties, and not being able to 'switch off'.

It is a good idea to try and relax before going to bed, make sure that you are not too cold, don't let your room get too stuffy, and don't go to bed hungry! If you have a lot of muscle/joint pain, a warm bath is often helpful, as well as an electric blanket!

2. *Diet*—many people with M.E. have found that a change in their diet is helpful. Some 'treatments' for M.E. can be very expensive, but modifying the diet isn't so bad! Unfortunately, if you read through all the literature on M.E. you will soon realize that the advice on what to eat (or not) is wide and varied—with some diets being so restrictive

that it becomes virtually impossible to maintain a healthy, well-balanced diet. If you find something that works then stick to it, but be careful—and, if necessary, take advice on the subject. So whilst there are no hard and fast rules, as no two people with M.E. have exactly the same problems, here are a few general suggestions:

Foods to Avoid:

Sugar and Other Refined Carbohydrates: All types of sugar; white flour, rice and pasta; and foods containing these things—white bread, cakes, biscuits, etc.

Processed Foods: Packaged foods; those containing additives, 'E' numbers, sugar, salt.

Coffee, Tea, Soft-Drinks, Chocolate: Herbal teas and decaffeinated drinks are O.K., otherwise limit the amount of caffeine-containing drinks to two or three a day.

Alcohol: Suicidal for anyone with M.E.!

Wheat/Gluten and Dairy Products: This does not apply to everyone, but some M.E. sufferers find that they cannot tolerate either one or both of these products.

Foods to Eat: Despite the list of foods to avoid,

it is still possible to maintain a balanced diet—which is probably more healthy than what you used to eat.

Fruit and Vegetables: Try to eat a lot of fresh fruit and vegetables, in order to maintain a good intake of vitamins and minerals. It is best to eat them raw, but if you do cook them steaming is better than boiling. Fruit and vegetables also help ensure a good intake of fibre—which is necessary to help digestion, and is also found in potatoes, unrefined flour, brown rice and pasta, and in oats.

Protein: An adequate protein intake is also needed. However many people with M.E. cannot tolerate red meat or dairy products—red meats are not particularly healthy anyway as they contain a lot of animal fat and are high in cholesterol. By cutting out red meats (although lamb can often be tolerated by those who cannot eat other red meats), and eating poultry, fish and eggs, a good supply of protein is maintained. Eggs also contain B vitamins, vitamins A and E, as well as zinc. Live yoghurt is also a source of protein, and contains 'good' bacteria which can help to lessen any bowel problems.

Complex Carbohydrates: Provide 'fuel' for the

body's energy. They are found in whole-wheat, potatoes, brown rice and pasta, and oats. They give a gradual rise in blood-sugar levels, instead of the rapid rise and fall of blood-sugar levels when eating refined carbohydrates such as sugar.

Fats: Try to avoid 'saturated' fats, as in red meats and diary products. Use olive or vegetable oils for cooking. Fish oils contain 'Essential Fatty Acids' which are needed to maintain normal function of the immune system, muscles and nerves. E.F.A.'s occur naturally in tuna, sardines and mackerel.

Vitamin Supplements: Many people with M.E. have found it helpful to take various vitamin supplements. Whilst taking high doses of vitamins is not always a good idea (unless given under medical supervision), certain individual vitamins can be helpful:

Vitamin A helps in building up resistance to infection.

B-complex vitamins help to provide energy for the body; help in the metabolism of fats; play a major role in the functioning of the nerves and nervous system; help to maintain healthy skin and digestion; are involved in the repair and regeneration of the liver, and in the production of red blood cells and haemoglobin.

Vitamin C is needed for repair and regeneration of body tissues; it also helps the immune system and is an anti-viral agent. It can be beneficial to take extra vitamin C when under stress or experiencing a secondary infection.

Vitamins A, C and E are anti-oxidants *i.e.* they protect against damage to body cells. Zinc is essential for the correct functioning of the body's enzyme systems and is important in maintaining a healthy immune system.

Vitamin and mineral supplements can be bought from chemists and health-food shops, and are also available from a number of places by mail order, *e.g.*

Nature's Best	Biocare
Century Place	Lakeside
Tunbridge Wells	180 Lifford Lane
Kent	Kings Norton
TN2 3BE	Birmingham
Tel: 01892 552176	B30 3NU
	Tel: 0121 433 3727

So the two main ways to help yourself manage

M.E. are Rest and Diet. It is also a good idea to have a hobby, if you can cope with it! Something that you can easily pick-up or put-down is probably best, *e.g.* using a computer or playing a musical instrument. Although rest is necessary, getting bored won't help!

It is helpful if you can learn to pace yourself, so that you do not over do it. Try to be aware of when you are getting near your limit. When you have a good day (they do exist!) avoid trying to do all the things you were not able to do the day before.

Try thinking of M.E. as being like having a large 'energy overdraft', and therefore in order to make progress you must never over-spend on energy! Rather, it is necessary never to push yourself too hard, reaching total exhaustion, as this will only prolong or worsen your condition. So, the sooner the illness is properly managed, the sooner progress is likely to be made.

Most of those who get M.E. were, before their illness, active and independent, not used to dealing with health problems—and suddenly having to cope with chronic ill-health poses quite a challenge! The Bible does not promise us reasons for why things happen to us—but we are assured that, if we are Christians, all things are for God's glory and our ultimate good (see Romans 8:17 & 28). It can be very frustrating to see things that need to be done, and be unable to do them—particularly in the sphere of church/Christian activities. Yet God knows our individual circumstances and will not expect us to do what we cannot physically manage.

But this doesn't mean that our Christian lives are of no use. For example, learning to manage and live with a serious illness can be a witness to those around us, particularly non-Christians—as we do not live in our own strength but through 'Christ Who strengthens me' (Philippians 4:13). JC Ryle commented that it is possible for those who are ill to 'honour God as much by patient suffering as they can by active work. It often shows more grace to sit still than it does to go to and fro, and perform great exploits.' '... In quietness and confidence shall be your strength' (Isaiah 30:15).

With an illness such as M.E., which is by its nature very isolating at times, it is important to maintain outside interests in order to prevent concentrating all the time on your own situation. There are some activities that can be done by those without much energy—and may open up a new sphere of interest or ministry.

One thing that I have enjoyed over the past few years is letterwriting—I currently correspond with a few people with M.E., as well as a number of missionaries/Christian workers in various parts of the World. It is a real privilege to hear of how God is at work in different countries and situations, and obviously this leads on to another area of work—prayer! You don't have to be at a Prayer Meeting to pray (although, if it is physically possible, keeping up attendance at a Prayer Meeting is recommended!). However, lying in bed is no barrier to prayer! Prayer-letters from missionaries are always helpful, as well as up-to-date needs from church, family, news items, etc., and will give plenty of 'fuel' for prayer.

Other available activities open to us include reading. As Christians, it is vitally important to keep up with daily Bible reading. This can be difficult, due to fatigue and lack of concentration—but stick at it! Following a Bible reading scheme and/or using some good reading notes can be helpful, as well as having a 'Quiet Time' at the same time each day. Reading other books is also good—and 'talking books' on cassette are often easier to cope with than the written variety!

If M.E. prevents attendance at some or all of the church services, it is usually possible to keep up with the services by listening to them on tape. One advantage of cassettes is that if you don't take in what is said the first time round, you can listen as many times as necessary! Some churches also have a 'Cassette Ministry', where anyone is welcome to borrow or buy tapes. For example, for some years I have been 'subscribing' to tapes of the Sunday services and weekly Bible studies from the Metropolitan Tabernacle, London, and have been greatly blessed and helped through this ministry.

The Metropolitan Tabernacle also has a good bookshop—and it is easy to order from it either online or by phone. Virtually all of the books that it sells are at lower prices than other Christian bookshops, due to bulk-buying. For further information contact:

Tabernacle Cassette Ministry/Bookshop
Metropolitan Tabernacle
Elephant & Castle
London
SE1 6SD
Tel: 020 7735 7076
Bookshop Website: www.tabernaclebookshop.org
Tabernacle Website: www.metropolitantabernacle.org

WHAT OTHER HELP IS AVAILABLE?

The best ways to help yourself, then, are rest and diet, as discussed previously. However outside help and support are available. There is not yet a cure for M.E., but there are various 'treatments', some of which could be worth trying. The main problem is that what works for one person will not necessarily work for the next, and many of the treatments are not available on the N.H.S. and can be expensive.

1 Treatments

a. *Magnesium Treatment:* Magnesium is the second most common mineral in our cells, and is necessary for normal muscle function. It occurs naturally in green vegetables, grains, nuts and soya. A study carried out in 1991 among a group of M.E. patients showed that many of their symptoms were similar to those found in people suffering from magnesium deficiency. The treatment involved a weekly injection of magnesium sulphate, injected intramuscularly, lasting for 6 weeks. The magnesium is best not taken in tablet form, as it is thought that most people with M.E. will not absorb it properly if taken orally.

In the study about 80% of sufferers improved: some benefited straight away; others needed to complete the course before feeling any real effect. However in follow-up trials the results haven't been quite so impressive!

The treatment is said to be without side-effects, as long as you have no history of heart or kidney problems. It should be available on the N.H.S. from your G.P., but if your G.P. doesn't know much about it he probably won't want to provide it—you will have to keep him informed! An information pack about Magnesium Treatment is available from *Action for M.E.,* which can be given to G.P.s. The treatment is available privately, but this would be expensive. It is not a cure for M.E., but if a blood test shows that magnesium deficiency is a problem for you, then it could well help. (If you have a blood test to look for magnesium deficiency, make sure it tests the red cell magnesium level, as this is the best indicator of any deficiency.)

b. *Anti-Candida Treatment:* Candida Albicans is a yeast which exists in the gut of all of us. In some people it gets out of hand, and needs to be bought under control. There are many factors that can cause the spread of Candida, including the over-use of antibiotics and steroids, and a diet high in sugar. Although Candida can be a problem in its own right, it would seem that many people with M.E. (some would say at least 50%) have some sort of Candida problem. Some blood tests are now available which can help to confirm a diagnosis of candida overgrowth (*e.g.* the 'Gut Fermentation Test'—not as bad as it sounds!), but are usually only available privately. Actually, the simplest way of determining whether or not you have a Candida problem is by treating it to see if you feel better!

The main part of any anti-Candida programme is to go on the anti-Candida diet.

This is a yeast and sugar free diet. All types of sugar and sugar-containing foods should be avoided; yeast and refined flours are also out; mouldy and fermented foods ought to be avoided as well. If you follow these measures, as well as the diet described in section two, then you should be well on the way to bringing any Candida problem under control.

However, in order to fully eliminate the problem, diet alone is not usually good enough, and some forms of anti-Candida medication are necessary. There are various anti-fungal drug treatments, for example Nystan and Fungilin. These are available on prescription, but you need a G.P. who has experience of using them. There are also some natural alternatives, for those who wish to avoid drugs, such as Caprylic Acid (available as Mycopryl from Biocare).

Following a strict anti-Candida diet and taking some anti-fungal medication should resolve any Candida problem. However, you really do need to find a doctor well experienced in treating the problem, and who has experience prescribing the various drugs available—which can be easier said than done!

If Candida is not a problem for you, then this diet won't have any effect—although the fact that it is a healthy diet may in itself help!

c. *Evening Primrose Oil:* Contains an Essential Fatty Acid called gamma-linolenic acid. E.F.A.s have an anti-viral effect, and are important for the proper functioning of the immune system, muscles and nerves. In a trial in Glasgow in 1990 85% of M.E. patients taking part showed some improvement—but they had to take a high dose of 6–8 x 500 mg Efamol Marine capsules (80% evening primrose oil/20% fish oil) a day for at least 3 months. There were no reports of any side-effects.

d. *Allergies and Food Intolerance:* Many people believe that problems with allergies and food intolerances can form a major part of M.E., as with Candida (in fact some would say that where Candida overgrowth is a problem, this can itself be the cause of many food and chemical intolerances). It is thought that over-use of antibiotics and slow recovery from viral illnesses (both of which are common in M.E.) can predispose a person to developing various allergies or intolerances—although in M.E. any problem is most likely to be due to an intolerance (which builds up over time) rather

43

than an allergy (which is usually a sudden, violent reaction).

The foods which most often pose problems for those with M.E. are wheat/gluten and dairy products, as well as caffeine and alcohol. Any such problems can usually be identified using an elimination diet—with the suspected 'culprits' being temporarily removed from the diet for a few days, and then reintroducing them one at a time to see if there is any reaction. Any 'problem' foods can then taken out of the diet. This may sound simple, but it can be difficult getting used to a restricted diet, particularly when you have very little energy to start with!

Soya and other non-milk alternatives can be used instead of dairy products, and are available from health food shops and some supermarkets.

If a gluten-free diet is necessary, it is advisable to contact Coeliac UK. They will require a signed doctors note confirming you have M.E. before allowing you to buy their publications. 'The Food List' is updated each year and gives detailed advice on which foods can be eaten. They also supply other information about living on a gluten-free diet.

For further information contact:

Coeliac UK
PO Box 220
High Wycombe
Buckinghamshire
HP11 2HY
Tel: 01494 437278
http://www.coeliac.co.uk

Gluten-free bread/cakes can be bought from health food shops, and are also available either online or by mail-order from:

Lifestyle Healthcare Ltd
Centenary Business Park
Henley-on-Thames
Oxfordshire
RG6 1DS
Tel: 01491 411767
http://www.glutenfree.co.uk/

Learning to cope with a diet that is different to what you are used to does take a bit of time, but is not too much of a problem when at home. The main difficulties can be when eating out— but there is normally something suitable available. Most people with M.E. would probably argue that it is worth sticking with a restrictive diet, as long as it is healthy and well-balanced, in order to relieve any of the symptoms of this frustrating illness!

If food and/or chemical sensitivities become a major problem (and some people with M.E. do seem to become intolerant of numerous foods and chemicals, which makes life extremely difficult), it would be advisable to get advice from a practitioner skilled in treating such conditions.

There are other 'treatments' available for M.E., but these are probably the four main ones. Other treatments include using anti-depressants to help restore normal sleep-patterns. However, they don't work for everyone with M.E., and some feel worse. The herbal remedy St John's Wort has been found to be as good as anti-depressants in treating both depression and sleep problems—and it doesn't result in all of the side-effects that can occur with orthodox medication.

There are also two main forms of complementary medicine—herbal medicine and homeopathy:

a. *Herbal Medicine*—Herbalism was the original form of medicine from which today's orthodox medicine developed. Therefore many modern drugs are derived from plants, and on the whole herbal medicines tend to be safer than synthetic drugs if used as prescribed. Many remedies are available at health food shops, but for a chronic condition such as M.E. it is a good idea to see a qualified medical herbalist. They will take a detailed history, and prescribe a herb or combination of herbs.

For further information contact:

National Institute of Medical Herbalists
56 Longbrook Street
Exeter
Devon
EX4 6AH
Tel: 01392 426022
http://www.nimh.org.uk/

However some people have tried treating themselves with various herbal remedies. Some herbs that have been found to be useful in M.E. are as follows:

Echinacea: for its anti-viral properties and support of the immune system.

Ginkgo Biloba: to improve circulation to the brain; can also help with dizziness.

St John's Wort: for support of the nervous system; also to aid the restoration normal sleeping patterns.

Feverfew: to alleviate and control migraine-type headaches.

b. *Homeopathy*—homeopathy follows the principle that 'like cures like'. A homeopathic remedy is a specially diluted preparation of a substance which, when taken by a healthy person, produces symptoms similar to those of the patient. The greater the dilution of the medicine, the more powerful it becomes. The curative effect comes from stimulation of the body to get rid of what is causing the symptoms. Homeopathy sees symptoms as the body's reaction against the illness as it attempts to overcome it, and therefore seeks to stimulate and not suppress this reaction.

Like herbal medicine, some homeopathic remedies are available in health food shops and chemists, but with an illness like M.E. it is worth seeing a fully trained medical homeopathist. A medical history is taken, along with details of personality, in order to build up a full picture of the problem. Remedies are prescribed to fit both the symptoms and the person—so different people with the same illness may all be prescribed different medication.

There are no side-effects from homeopathy (although an aggravation of symptoms can occur at first), and it is safe for children to use.

For further information contact:

British Homeopathic Association
Hahnemann House, 29 Park Street West
Luton
LU1 3BE
Tel: 0870 444 3950
http://www.trusthomeopathy.org

All members of the B.H.A. are medically trained homeopathic practitioners.

I have mentioned herbal medicine and homeopathy because I believe that they are complementary to orthodox medicine. Both forms of treatment have been subjected to various scientific trials showing their effectiveness in treating a variety of conditions.

There are also numerous types of 'alternative' therapies which many people have found to be beneficial *e.g.* acupuncture, yoga, reiki, shiatsu. However, just about all of the 'alternative' treatments seem to have a link with false religion and/or the New Age movement, and should therefore be avoided by Christians (cf. Ephesians 5:11: 'And have no fellowship with the unfruitful works of darkness, but rather expose them.'). Care is even needed when considering herbal or homeopathic medicine, to make sure that the practitioner is properly medically qualified—as even these forms of treatment have been 'hijacked' by some and incorporated into the alternative/New Age sphere.

It should also be noted that some alternative treatments involve an altered level of consciousness (*e.g.* hypnotherapy, Transcendental Meditation)—and this is something clearly forbidden in Scripture, where we are told to remain rational, alert, and in control of our minds *e.g.* 2 Timothy 1:7: 'For God has not given us a spirit of fear, but of power and of love and of a *sound mind [self-control* (N.I.V.)]'; 2 Peter 1:5–6: 'But also for this very reason, giving all diligence, add to your faith virtue, to virtue knowledge, to knowledge *self-control,* to *self-control* perseverance (patience), to perseverance godliness.'

Whatever you decide to do, remember: there is no cure for M.E., and some sufferers have spent a lot of time, money and energy trying to find one. If you do decide to try out some form of treatment, do make sure that the practitioner is medically qualified and has experience of treating people with M.E.!

Also, remember that Christians who are living with a chronic illness are in the unique position of being able to help others (both Christians and non-Christians) in similar situations: 2 Corinthians 1:3–4: 'Blessed be the God and Father of our Lord Jesus Christ, the Father of mercies and God of all comfort, Who comforts us in all our tribulation, that we may be able to comfort those who are in any trouble (tribulation), with the comfort with which we ourselves are comforted by God.'

2 Support

If you have M.E. then you will need support. There are two organizations which provide support and information for M.E. sufferers and their families:

a. *The M.E. Association*—founded in 1976, the M.E. Association became a registered charity in 1980. It is now a large, professionally run organization, and has a nationwide network of self-help groups and a listening ear helpline. It has 3 main aims: to offer support to people with M.E.; to spread information about the illness; and to promote research. It produces a magazine, *Perspectives,* four times a year and numerous leaflets on M.E.-related issues, as well as funding various research programmes. The organization campaigns for more government recognition of M.E. and aims to send information to all G.P.s. The Association has an orthodox medical approach to M.E. Membership is £15 per year.

For further information contact:

The M.E. Association
4 Top Angel
Buckingham Industrial Park
Buckingham
Buckinghamshire
MK18 1TH
http://www.meassociation.org.uk/

b. *Action for M.E.*—Action for M.E. (formerly Action for M.E and Chronic Fatigue) was founded in 1987 to give help and information to people with M.E. It now has over 7,000 members. It also funds research, and campaigns for M.E. to be properly recognised. Action for M.E. accepts orthodox, complementary and alternative medical approaches to M.E.

The charity produces a journal, *Interaction,* four times a year, as well as various leaflets and factsheets, including some designed for young children, teenagers, school teachers, families and friends of sufferers, and G.P.s. They have a telephone helpline and a number of support groups nationwide. They have also produced a 'Therapy Information Pack', giving details of therapies/treatments which some people have found helpful. Membership is £15 per year.

For further information contact:

Action for M.E.
PO Box 1302
Wells
Somerset
BA5 1YE
Tel: 01749 670799
Fax: 01749 672561
http://www.afme.org.uk/

I would say that it is worth joining either one or both of these charity organizations, as they will keep you up-to-date with the latest information on M.E., and they provide lists of contacts so that you can get in touch with other sufferers. It is a good idea to keep family and friends up-to-date on M.E. as well, so that they will know how best to help you. You may also find that it is up to you to keep your G.P. informed on the latest news on M.E., as you will probably know more about it than he does!

WHY DOES GOD ALLOW
US TO SUFFER?

Many people ask 'Why does God allow us to suffer?' or 'Shouldn't Christians be free from suffering?' As a Christian I believe that to find the answer we need to look at what the Bible says on the subject. The book of Job is concerned with human suffering. Job does not know the reason for his suffering, but is content to know that God is in control and to put his trust in God.

The Bible teaches that God often speaks to us, and to those around us, through suffering. Through times of suffering we realise how weak we are, and how totally dependent we are on God. We learn that we can trust in the promises of the Bible, knowing that God is sovereign and He only lets us suffer as much as we can endure; and that He has promised to give us the strength to meet all our needs—and that includes M.E.! We are always in His hand and kept 'under the shadow of the Almighty' (Psalm 91:1).

Yet, while it is true that God has promised to supply all our needs (Philippians 4:19), I don't believe that He gives us the strength that we require in advance—because we are told that 'the just shall live by faith' (Romans 1:17), and that His mercies 'are new every morning' (see Lamentations 3:22–23). Therefore we need to trust Him to give us each day the grace and strength to cope with the situations that we are faced with.

An encouraging text for anyone facing difficulties is Jeremiah 32:17: 'Ah, Lord God! Behold, You have made the heavens and the earth by Your great power and outstretched arm. There is nothing too hard for You.' Our God is the One Who by His Word alone created the entire Universe—therefore nothing is too difficult for Him or outside of His control. If it be His will He can heal us; if not, He has promised to give us all that we need to manage day by day.

Some believe that Christians should be free from illness and pain, but we live in a fallen world where there will always be sickness and suffering, and it is an inescapable part of our lives. However, it is true that, 'the God of providence has limited the time, manner, intensity, repetition and effects of all our sicknesses. The limit is also wisely adjusted to our strength—we cannot suffer too much or be relieved too late. The thought is full of consolation that He Who has fixed the bounds of our habitation has also fixed the bounds of our tribulation' (C.H. Spurgeon).

God sometimes uses terrible circumstances, when people are at their lowest, to bring them to Himself; and there are many Christians who have suffered terribly, yet their lives are an encouragement to others who suffer and a challenge to those who are not Christians.

When considering what the Bible says about suffering, the following comment by Peter Masters in his book *The Healing Epidemic* is very helpful:

No trial, affliction or sickness is to be regarded as an accident or a totally purposeless nuisance. It is right to seek immediate medical help and to pray for healing. It is wrong to lose patience and to throw away the promise—*that all things work together for good to them that love God.* To summarise, we are taught in James 5 that for both categories of suffering—external troubles and in bodily illnesses—the following attitudes should be adopted by believers:

1 We must expect them both.

2 We must pray for help and deliverance.

3 We must be prepared to exercise patience, for God may strengthen us to bear the problem rather than take it away.

4 We must believe that a problem not removed serves a purpose which will work to our eternal good, and may stand as a witness to others.

(Dr Peter Masters, *The Healing Epidemic,* The Wakeman Trust pp. 143–144; used with permission).

Reasons For Suffering—far from being immune to suffering, the Bible teaches that, as Christians, we should expect to suffer. Scripture gives many reasons for suffering, some of which I have listed:

Chastisement

For whom the Lord loves He corrects, just as a father the son in whom he delights (Proverbs 3:12).

... so that through them I may test Israel, whether they will keep the ways of the Lord, to walk in them as their fathers kept them, or not (Judges 2:22).

Testing/Purifying

For You, O God, have tested us; You have refined us as silver is refined (Psalm 66:10).

... knowing that the testing of your faith produces patience ... Blessed is the man who endures temptation [*trial* (N.I.V.)]; for when he has been approved, he will receive the crown of life which the Lord has promised to those who love Him (James 1:3 & 12).

In this you greatly rejoice, though now for a little while, if need be, you have been grieved by various trials, that the genuineness of your faith, being much more precious than gold that perishes, though it is tested by fire, may be found to praise, honour, and glory, at the revelation of Jesus Christ, Whom having not seen you love (1 Peter 1:6–8a).

And not only that, but we also glory in tribulations, knowing that tribulation produces perseverance; and perseverance, character; and character, hope (Romans 5:3–4).

To Become More Dependent on God

Before I was afflicted I went astray, but now I keep Your Word (Psalm 119:67).

Who shall separate us from the love of Christ? Shall tribulation, or distress, or persecution, or famine, or nakedness, or peril, or sword? As it is written: 'For Your sake we are killed all day long; we are accounted as sheep for the slaughter' (Romans 8:35–36).

Learning to Know the Presence of Christ in All Circumstances

Yea, though I walk through the valley of the shadow of death, I will fear no evil; For You are with me; Your rod and Your staff, they comfort me (Psalm 23:4).

If I take the wings of the morning, And dwell in the uttermost parts of the sea, Even there Your hand shall lead me, And Your right hand shall hold me (Psalm 139:9–10).

BUT

And we know that all things work together for good to those who love God, to those who are the called according to His purpose. For whom He foreknew, He also predestined to be conformed to the image of His Son, that He might be the firstborn among many brethren (Romans 8:28–29).

And He said to me, 'My grace is sufficient for you, for My strength is made perfect in weakness' (2 Corinthians 12:9).

I can do all things through Christ Who strengthens me (Philippians 4:13).

Yet in all these things we are more than conquerors through Him Who loved us. For I am persuaded that neither death nor life, nor angels nor principalities nor powers, nor things present nor things to come, nor height nor depth, nor any other created thing, shall be able to separate us from the love of God which is in Christ Jesus our Lord (Romans 8:37–39).

The sufferings of Christians should always make them develop a stronger dependence on God and a more Christ-like character—'Now no chastening [discipline (N.I.V.)] seems to be joyful for the present, but painful;

nevertheless, afterward it yields the peaceable fruit of righteousness to those who have been trained by it' (Hebrews 12:11).

Although we face suffering and the effects of a fallen world here on earth, we have hope. We know that a time is coming when 'God will wipe away every tear from their eyes; there shall be no more death, nor sorrow, nor crying. There shall be no more pain, for the former things have passed away' (Revelation 21:4). Hallelujah!

'There is comfort for the bereft soul, for the sore stricken spirit, and for those who in their bodies are bearing the burdens of weakness, and disease and suffering—the comfort that when Jesus comes we shall enter into the completeness of redemption won for us on Calvary' (J Russell Howden).

'Do you not know? Have you not heard? The Lord is the everlasting God, the Creator of the ends of the earth. He will not grow tired or weary, and His understanding no one can fathom. He gives strength to the weary and increases the power of the weak. Even the youths grow tired and weary, and young men stumble and fall; but those who hope in the Lord will renew their strength. They will soar on wings like eagles; they will run and not grow weary, they will walk and not be faint.'

ISAIAH 40:28–31 (N.I.V.)

ON EAGLES' WINGS

The verses of Scripture that have been particularly special to me since being ill are Isaiah 40:28–31. It is not our physical strength or abilities that really count—it is putting our faith, hope and trust in the Lord. Then, as a result, we can look beyond our problems (however real and frustrating they may be!), knowing that we are in His care, under His shadow, and will ultimately be with Him in Glory. His everlasting arms are always underneath us (Deuteronomy 33:27); His everlasting love always surrounds us.

It is an interesting fact that when an eagle flies into a storm it tilts its wings, which enables it to soar upwards and thereby fly over the storm. This is of course a lesson and encouragement for us—to look to the Lord to guide us through, and over, whatever the circumstances are that we find ourselves in.

POSTSCRIPT

I hope that the information in this book will be of some help to you. I am not medically qualified in any way. The book is designed to give general information only, and is in no way a substitute for medical advice. I cannot recommend or endorse any particular treatment, and different people respond to different things anyway. If in doubt, seek the advice of a doctor before trying anything new. The advice given is simply what I have learnt from my own experiences of having M.E. I have tried to include the details of M.E. that I would like to have known at the beginning of my illness and to include some practical advice. I realise that there are varying views on M.E. and how to treat it, but I can only write what I believe to be correct.

I also pray that it might encourage you to hope in the Lord however difficult your situation may be.

Hazel Stapleton.

FURTHER READING

M.E.—Post Viral Fatigue Syndrome—How To Live With It, Dr Anne MacIntyre, Thorsons Books

Living With M.E.—A Self-help Guide, Dr Charles Shepherd, Vermillion

Why M.E.?, Dr Belinda Dawes and Dr Damien Downing, Grafton Books

Better Recovery from Viral Illness, Dr Darrel Ho-Yen, Dodona Books

Finding Strength in Weakness, Lynn Vanderzalm, Zondervan

Complete Guide to Food Allergy and Intolerance, Dr Jonathan Brostoff and Linda Gamlin, Bloomsbury Press

Candida Albicans—Could Yeast Be Your Problem?, Leon Chaitow, Thorsons Books

When God's Children Suffer, Horatius Bonar, Kregal Publications

Sickness and Death in the Christian Family, Peter Jeffery, Evangelical Press

Comfort For Christians, AW Pink, Baker Book House

The Sovereignty of God, AW Pink, Banner of Truth

A Path Through Suffering, Elisabeth Elliot, OM Publishing

Deserted By God? Sinclair Ferguson, Banner of Truth

The Bumps Are What You Climb On— Encouragement For Difficult Days, Warren Wiersbe, Crossway Books

Secret Strength, Joni Eareckson-Tada, Multonomah Press

The Healing Epidemic, Peter Masters, The Wakeman Trust

Charismatic Chaos, John MacArthur, Zondervan

The Signs and Wonders Movement: Exposed,
Editor: Peter Glover, Day One Publications

Also available from Quinta Press

The Works of George Whitefield, CD-ROM

The text of the Works of George Whitefield published in 1771 along with images of the pages of the original Works, additional letters and sermons, Whitefield's Tabernacle Hymn Book, biographies by Gillies, Tyerman, Andrews, Philips and Gledstone, a collection of Anecdotes by Wakeley and a collection of pictures and photographs are available in Adobe Acrobat PDF (Portable Document Format) on CD-ROM suitable for Apple Macintosh, Linux and Windows 95 (and above) computers. It is planned that a fuller edition of Whitefield's Works, which requires more research to find additional material not originally included, will be published in the future.

Christian Fellowship or the Church Member's Guide
by John Angell James, 64pp booklet

How should churches be organised? How should church members relate to one another; to their minister; to other churches? In this book, John Angell James answers these and other questions from a biblical perspective. Its purpose is clearly described in its sub-title *The Church Member's Guide*. Writing from an Independent/Congregational background James' words are not restricted by narrow denominationalism but are relevant to all churches which seek to practise Biblical church fellowship. If the principles of this book are applied, it will result in closer Christian fellowship within churches and between churches. The text of this volume has been abridged by Gordon Booth in order to remove the wordiness of the Victorian original and make it available to a modern readership. This book is suitable for group study and pastors can be encouraged to use it as a study guide for church members.

The Anxious Inquirer
by John Angell James, paperback

This book was widely read during the 19th century and was the means by which a great many people came to a true faith in Jesus Christ for salvation. While the dated language makes it unsuitable for general use today it gives an excellent example to Christians of how to counsel unbelievers who are seeking salvation.

Anecdotes of George Whitefield
by J.B. Wakeley, hardback

A brief biography and a collection of anecdotes of the great preacher of the 18th century. These anecdotes give insights into Whitefield's life and attitudes not available in most biographies.

Church Establishments
by Henry Birch, paperback

When this book was published in 1872 the disestablishment of the Church of England as the church 'by law established' (which the monarch vowed to uphold and maintain at her coronation) was a major issue. As a result, the Church of Ireland was disestablished. Irish home rule issues continued to take up parliamentary time and disestablishment was pushed off of the political agenda.

Nonetheless, as a result of a religious census in Wales, the Church of Wales was disestablished in 1921. Today many still argue that the Church of England should not be disestablished. A variety of arguments are used, including that it would result in the spiritual and moral decline of England. But disestablishment in Wales has happened and Wales is no worse than England. Henry Birch goes through all the biblical and practical reasons why establishment of religion is a bad thing and should be abandoned. The majority of his arguments are still valid today.

In Preparation

The Life and Letters of John Angell James

After his death, John Angell James' incomplete autobiography was published by RW Dale (his successor as the minister of Carr's Lane Congregational Church, Birmingham) with editorial comments. Another edition of the autobiography (also with editorial comments) was published by James's son as volume 17 of the Works of John Angell James. Quinta Press plans to publish a new edition of the autobiography combining these two editions in 2002. In the longer term it is hoped that a new edition of his complete works will also be published.

Christ the Fountain of Life by John Cotton

One of the leaders of New England Puritanism in the 17th century, Cotton's writings were highly influential in Britain and America. His writings on church government, especially *The Keys of the Kingdom of Heaven* (in preparation by Quinta Press) laid the foundation for the independent or congregational system of church government. *Christ the Fountain of Life* is a collection of sermons preached by Cotton on 1 John 5.

A more up to date list of books available
can be viewed at the Quinta Press web-site,
www.quintapress.com.